MW01591230

Jordan's Journeys

A (NOT) SO SILENT CHRISTMAS

★ an apraxia story ★

written by:
Jordan Christian LeVan

illustrations by:
Sydney J. Stone

Jordan's Journeys

A (NOT) SO SILENT CHRISTMAS

★ an apraxia story ★

Illustrations by: Sydney J. Stone

ISBN: 978-1-961783-03-4 (pbk)

"My wish this Christmas
is that everyone feels heard and understood,
even those who cannot speak yet."

Jordan was
so excited for Christmas
this year.

Spoken words couldn't capture the joy.

Every year,
Jordan and his sister
dragged the tree up
the stairs.

Jordan and his siblings were preparing
for Santa Claus to come,

And when he did,

they knew he would be as quiet as a mouse.

Other family members mistook Jordan as quiet, like Santa Claus.

Because speaking was difficult.

However,
this was not a choice.

Jordan has apraxia of speech,

which makes it difficult for him to say
what he wants to say.

Later that year,

they would go to the mall to see Santa Claus.

And Jordan would sit on Santa's lap.

He would try
to tell him
what he wanted
this year.

But Santa's face
would look confused.

Jordan would look at his mom because he knew in his heart,

She knew he had a lot he wanted to say.

Mom helped him say what he wanted.

She brought store catalogs
so Jordan could point at what he wanted.

On Christmas day, they would go to family events

and he was so happy
to see everyone.

The adults around him
would tell others
how shy and quiet he was.

While Jordan would think,
"Why aren't you speaking to me?
I can still hear you."

This showed Jordan
they truly didn't
understand him
or the person he was.

Nobody should feel misunderstood
or unheard during such a glorious time of year.

All that Jordan ever wanted

Is to feel how his mom and siblings
made him feel,

those holiday years.

A Letter For Santa Claus

Dear Santa,

I am so excited to see you this holiday year!
My name is _____, and I am _____ years old.
I have difficulties speaking; however, I am still excited
to speak with you! Please include me and talk to me
like any other child because I have A LOT I want this
Christmas, and I have A LOT to say!

Thank you, Santa,
for bringing me so much cheer this holiday year.

decorate your stocking

Author Biography

Jordan Christian LeVan, a passionate advocate for apraxia, disability, and mental health, holds a Bachelor of Arts in Psychology, specializing in Mental Health Studies, from Guilford College in Greensboro, North Carolina.

He shares his personal journey with Verbal Apraxia through his blog "Fighting for my Voice: My Life with Verbal Apraxia."

As the Founder and President of
The Apraxia Foundation: Hearing All Voices, Inc.
Jordan's mission is to promote inclusivity, celebrate diversity, and foster global understanding and acceptance.

For more resources, visit his blog at Fightingformyvoice.com
and connect on Facebook at Facebook.com/fightingformyvoice.

Printed in the USA
CPSIA information can be obtained
at www.ICGtesting.com
LVHW082255301123
765241LV00016B/444